Kingdom Journey

Becoming More Aware of Our Spiritual Reality

By

Tess Gillaspy

TABLE OF CONTENTS

Introduction

If you are reading this book, then you are experiencing a victory that has been over ten years in the making. It was very clear to me that God wanted me to write this book. It was an assignment that would never let me go. Over ten years of prodding, in fact. There were many false starts, but this time I knew it had to happen. Why? Because a large part of the 21st century church is not walking and acting upon the kingdom power that is available to her. He said I was to write about living in His Kingdom and what that looked like from my perspective. Now is the appointed time, and this is the season.

We are spiritual beings existing for a short time in a physical body. Before I invited Jesus into my life, I was only aware of my life in the physical sense. If I felt hungry, I ate. If I was sad, I cried. My entire world was wrapped up in what my five senses could experience and what I thought or felt. There was no other plane of existence – until Jesus. Even then, I was like a baby learning a new skill – to be aware of a spiritual dimension was something that had to be learned. New habits formed. I became intentional in focusing my mind on what was happening in the Kingdom of God or the spiritual realm around me. Just because I could not see it did not mean it didn't exist.

How many can distinguish the voice of God in their mind? How many of us talk with Him throughout our day? How many of us act on the daily instructions He gives? There are not enough of us aware of the Kingdom of Heaven around us. Our effectiveness in this season is determined by our communication with our Father through the Holy Spirit.

This is not a game we are playing. I am not here to teach you a new trick. We are living in the Church Age. This is the time for us to stand up and take our place in the battle between good and evil. Jesus gave us the keys that can loose and bind things here on earth and in the heavenly realm.

Matthew 16:19 *I will give you the keys of the kingdom of heaven; whatever you bind on earth will be bound in heaven, and whatsoever you loose on earth will be loosed in heaven.*

Very few people in the church know how to use these

keys that Jesus is talking about. I pray this book will show you what is possible.

Maybe your relationship with God is a close and intimate one, but you have yet to say "yes" to an assignment that is uniquely yours. Or maybe you have been discouraged and your faith has been bruised and trampled. Either way, it's time to lean in, family.

We will explore exactly what the Kingdom of God is and how we access it here while we live our lives on earth. It is also important to be clear about WHY we should be exercising our ability to walk in the spiritual dimension as well as the physical if we are to be useful to God in this life.

How do we accomplish this? So many of us have existed our entire lives on one plane of existence. We know no other way of life.

In this book I share personal accounts of my own encounters with the Holy Spirit. I will describe how these accounts came about and the outcome. I like to tell stories and I like listening to your stories. This book includes some of my stories and lessons learned. I pray your journey will be enriched by it. I pray it mobilizes us all in the way God intended.

Chapter One:
What is the Kingdom of God?

Before we ever delve into how to live in the Kingdom of God, it is vital that we have a grasp of what that actually is. How can we achieve something that is spiritual? It can feel out of reach – over my head. It's simple – like all Godly concepts – but not always easy.

> Luke 17:20-21 ...*the coming of the kingdom of God is not something that can be observed. Nor will people say, 'here it is' or 'there it is', because the kingdom of God is within you*

The indwelling Holy Spirit gives us access to God's Kingdom. He is the door we walk through to experience God's heavenly kingdom. We must examine this more to get a good picture. When we are born again and come to accept Jesus as our Lord and Savior, our spirit comes alive in a new way. The Kingdom of God is where we will now spend eternity. It is our eternal existence. Our spirits have always been eternal. Every human spirit will exist for eternity in either heaven (the Kingdom of God) or hell. The duality of our existence is between what we experience in the physical and what we experience in the spiritual. I can be sitting at my desk, like I am now, and God can show me a vision of maybe angels hovering – protecting me as I stay on task. If we are going to spend the rest of eternity in the Kingdom of God, we should get familiar with our surroundings, don't you think? It's all a faith walk.

> 2 Corinthians 5:7 *For we live by faith not by sight.*

When you came to Christ, there was probably nothing tangible that confirmed you were now saved. The first time you "heard" God's voice you could have determined it was only your own mind giving you that thought, but something inside you chose to believe that it was God planting that thought in your head - faith it was Him and not you. So, when you sense that God is showing you or speaking a concept to you, you are experiencing His Kingdom.

Our existence is actually lived on two different planes simultaneously: the physical plane and spiritual plane.

I am not a science fiction fanatic, but I have enjoyed some movies made in the genre. It fascinates me when a story delves into existence in more than one dimension. Can a person exist in more than one dimension? I am writing this book to not only say you can, but we already do. God created us in His image according to Genesis 1:26. *Then God said, Let US make man in Our image, after our likeness.*

God is a three-part God – God the Father, God the Son, and God the Holy Spirit – all God but three distinct persons with different purposes. A human being is comprised of three parts also. Everyone has a body (the physical), a soul (mind, will and emotions) and a spirit (that which is eternal – either eternally saved or eternally damned). It is our soul and spirit that can exist in two dimensions simultaneously. When our being is aligned properly, with our spirit in charge of our soul and body, our spirit can utilize our mind, will, and emotions to connect with God in another realm – the Kingdom of God.

> Mark 4:11 *To you it has been given to know the mystery of the kingdom of God.*
>
> Luke 12:32 *Do not fear little flock for it is your Father's good pleasure to give you the kingdom.*

Let me give you some examples of when this takes place. We Christians like to pursue what we call "a quiet time" or a time devoted to God. We tend to fill this time with Bible study, devotionals and journaling our thoughts toward God. Lately, I have been cultivating a habit of giving God the "first fruits" of my day. Upon waking, I refuse to pick up my cell phone for the first hour of my day. I do the most mundane things during this hour like making coffee or giving my dog treats – all the while carrying on a conversation with God. I might take my coffee to my desk (the computer stays turned off). At my desk I read scripture and journal anything that jumps out at me that may be significant. God has met me here and transported me to the plane where He resides. Dwight L Moody[1] says it this way: *We talk about heaven being so far away. It is within speaking distance to those who belong there. Heaven is a prepared place for a prepared people.*

It is that dimension outside of time where God resides with two thirds of the angels He created. It is marked by indescribable beauty. It is eternal and now, as a believer, it is within you because His Spirit is within you.

Dutch Sheets shared his views on the Kingdom of God in his daily blog, *Give Him 15*,[2] quoting Ephesians 1:3, 1:20, 2:6, 3:10 and 6:12, *Blessed be the God and Father of our Lord Jesus Christ, who has blessed us with every spiritual blessing in THE HEAVENLY PLACES in Christ, which He brought about in Christ when He raised Him from the dead and seated Him at His right hand in THE HEAVENLY PLACES. And raised US up with Him and seated US with Him in the HEAVENLY PLACES, in Christ Jesus, so that the manifold wisdom of God might now be made known THROUGH THE CHURCH to the rulers and the authorities in the heavenly places. For our struggle is not against flesh and blood, but against the rulers, against powers, against world forces of this darkness, against the spiritual forces of wickedness in THE HEAVENLY PLACES.*

In 2 Kings 6:16-17 When the servant of the man of God got up and went out early the next morning, an army with horses and chariots had surrounded the city. 'Oh no, my Lord! What shall we do?' the servant asked.

'Don't be afraid,' the prophet answered, 'Those who are with us are more than those who are with them.'

And Elisha prayed, 'Open his eyes, Lord, so that he may see.' Then the Lord opened the servant's eyes, and he looked and saw the hills full of horses and chariots of fire all around Elisha.

Let's consider this realm. It not only refers to heaven, God's home, but to all the invisible, spiritual realm around us. We must consider this relatively unknown dimension to fully partner with God and experience the fullness of His blessing. It is the unseen realm of the spirit – invisible yet real, hidden yet very active, that we now place our focus.

PRAY WITH ME: *Father in heaven, I ask You to open my eyes and ears to Your kingdom. Help me to see and learn to exist in this spiritual realm with You. Do not allow the enemy of my soul to rob me of this opportunity to have a more intimate relationship with You. Let our communication be so clear that I am able to fulfill my destiny here on earth.*

DECREE AND DECLARE: *Every day I will learn to discern the voice of God and become familiar with walking in His spiritual kingdom.*

A Good Neighbor

It was a bright sunny late afternoon. I was talking to my neighbor over our shared fence. We would talk a lot about God. We liked sharing any new concept that we had learned or how God had made Himself known to us that day. She was sharing how God had told her what to buy and what not to buy at the store that morning. I was intrigued. I had been a Christian for over a decade at that point. I had sensed God's presence on numerous occasions, but I couldn't remember having conversations with Him.

I asked her "How did you hear Him telling you that?" She answered me with a question. "Don't you hear Him instructing you?" "Not really" I answered. She looked at me shocked and horrified. "Well, the Bible says My sheep know My voice. How can you be His sheep if you don't hear His voice?" Wow! Was I even saved?

I walked away from that fence that day with a lot to think about. Deciding that hearing God speak to me was just like every other thing I had asked God to do in my life – I knew it was time to ask. After all, it's a faith walk, right? I asked Him to be my Savior and determined to believe He had saved me. When I asked Him to fill me with His Spirit, I chose to believe He did and I was filled. Now, I wanted Him to allow me to recognize His voice. I needed to distinguish His voice from my own thoughts or the lies the enemy's whispers. Knowing the parameters that would guide me – that He would never say anything contrary to His Word – I asked Him to speak to me. The first words I remember Him speaking were, "Hello, Daughter!" Not exactly a profound Biblical truth but not unbiblical. He said it rather jauntily and upbeat. It was almost as if He was excited that I was finally listening. Here is the important part: I CHOSE to believe it was Him speaking to me.

Over the next few weeks and months, I began to listen for His voice and recognize it as His. I got pretty good at recognizing when it was Him speaking by first testing the thought by the Bible. It was as if He would speak and then plant the scripture in my head that confirmed it. Of course, for Him to be able to do that, you must study His

Word and know it in order for the Holy Spirit to bring it up.

I am so very grateful to my good neighbor who cared enough to challenge me to go deeper. Every one of us has a unique relationship with God. He will speak to you in a way that is different than the way He speaks to me. Kingdom living depends on our relationship and communication with the Father. Maybe your gifts do not include visions and dreams. Maybe public speaking is not part of your wheelhouse. Whatever the Lord has ordained as your destiny will involve communicating closely with Him. Talk to Him. Listen for Him. He is always speaking. We are not always listening.

Chapter Two:
Why is learning to dwell in the invisible Kingdom important?

As followers of Jesus to be effective here on earth, we must become familiar and even adept in functioning in these HEAVENLY PLACES.

Dutch Sheets goes on to say, *Surprisingly, most American Christians live their lives without weighing how much this realm affects us, let alone how we can operate in and influence it. Two invisible kingdoms working to control the world – angelic and demonic forces engaged in phenomenal warfare (2 Kings 6:15-18). We live in a world filled with constant angelic and demonic activity. Our natural eyes, however, cannot perceive it.*[2]

Many Christians still have a problem consciously relating to it. We believers must move beyond our fear of criticism and agree with Scripture. Jesus is our example and He frequently dealt with the invisible. He was aware of it and consistently engaged with unseen entities, stirring up demonic opposition everywhere He went. He released His spiritual authority into this realm through His words and actions.

The early church in Acts also did so, releasing Spirit-led decrees and confronting forces of darkness when appropriate. We are inconsistent if we confess to be Bible-believing followers of Christ and yet refuse to acknowledge and operate in the invisible realm. Failure in this area has rendered us largely impotent.

In their book "Releasing the Prophetic Destiny of a Nation," Dutch Sheets and Chuck Pierce state, *The more we learn to function in the invisible spiritual reality, recognizing and applying its governing principles, the more we can partner with God, positively impact our world, avoid the snares and influence of the evil one, and enjoy the blessings of our salvation.*[3]

One of my frequent prayers for my children and me is that we would become the people God created us to be and that we would fulfill our God-given destinies. We cannot do that by only functioning in the physical realm.

So much of what we see is influenced and governed by what we cannot see. I wear glasses. As I become more and more vintage, I need my glasses to see clearly. The Holy Spirit is, in a way, our corrective lenses into the heavenly or spiritual realm.

Throughout the book of Ephesians, Paul writes how we have everything we need to operate in heavenly places. Christ has been given all authority in this realm. We have been legally seated there with Him in His position of authority. Through us, from our position there with Christ, God intends to defeat the kingdom of darkness.

> Luke 12:32 *Do not fear little flock for it is your Father's good pleasure to give you the kingdom.*

We shouldn't sit idly and not pursue the knowledge of the spiritual realm and learn how to function there. To advance the Kingdom of God, we must become very proficient in living an existence of duality – existing in both the physical world and functioning in the spiritual realm. In chapter three we will discuss just how this can be accomplished.

PRAY WITH ME: *Lord, cause a deep understanding to grow in my heart as to why You have ordained us to this dual existence. Stir us up, God. Help us to experience the urgency of this season. Grow us up, Father, so we might run this race alongside You and finish well.*

DECREE AND DECLARE: *We will mature and grow proficient at working within the Kingdom of God so His will be done here and now.*

The Rescue

I found Jesus or He found me when I was almost 19 years old. I loved having a savior and plunged head first into church life. Twenty years later I couldn't find one Bible in my house. Somehow, I embraced Jesus as my Savior but never got around to making Him my Lord. Consequently, I made some extremely bad choices. I married an abusive alcoholic and my life spiraled out of control. One bad decision on top of another was burying me alive. It was as if when I got saved, I had received a huge golden present and after admiring it, placed it on a high shelf in my closet. I hadn't opened it to see what God had for me. I had no idea He had bestowed gifts to me or that surrender was the road to success in life.

One night I found myself trapped in my bedroom while my husband loomed over me with a knife. He kept saying he was going to kill me and I believed him. Praying in tongues under my breath I remember thinking that this may very well be the way my life came to an end. Suddenly, he shifted his stance and moved farther into the room leaving the path to the door clear. In my mind I heard an urgent message. "RUN!" I obediently jumped up without another thought and raced for the door and freedom. Outside I could hear the sirens of police coming to my aid. If I had not heard and obeyed the Holy Spirit telling me to move, the police would have been too late.

That night I learned the importance of immediate obedience.

Chapter Three:
How do we learn to live in the Kingdom of God?

We learn the skill of living in the Kingdom of God like we learn any other skill: practice. In Brother Lawrence's book "Practicing the Presence of God"[5], he gives us very practical instructions on how to dwell in God's presence all day, every day: *In order to know God, we must often think of Him, and when we come to love Him, we shall then also think of Him often, for our heart will be with our treasure.*

We practice being aware of Him. We talk to Him throughout our day and **listen** for His replies. As I stated earlier, God is always speaking, but we are not always listening. All relationships need attention. They all need time and communication. Marriages and friendships do not survive and grow in intimacy if they are never nurtured. It has to be intentional. Don't forget: we are spiritual beings living in a physical body, not the other way around.

> John 3: 3 Jesus replies, *Very truly I tell you, no one can see the Kingdom of God unless they are born from above.*

Before we became believers and disciples of Jesus, we only knew one plane of existence. It is only after our spirits are born anew that we can venture into the God's realm and establish a personal relationship with Him. Then we can hear Him, see things from His perspective, receive visions and dreams, and enter into the abundant life He promises.

Where can we practice? We start by being intentional and aware during a time set aside for just us and God every day. I also find that time driving alone is a wonderful opportunity to practice awareness of God's presence with me.

> Hebrews 4:16 *Let us then approach God's throne of grace with confidence, so that we may receive mercy and find grace to help us in our time of need.*

Alone time with Jesus is vital but corporate worship is another opportunity to encounter God in powerful ways. Holy Spirit is present and eager to speak wisdom, direction and love into our lives when we are in church. He may speak to us through a song, through the sermon, communion or even through a conversation with another believer.

When we choose to be intentionally aware of Him throughout our day, our relationship grows and our ability to see how we exist in the Kingdom of God as well as on earth becomes second nature to us.

> Colossians 3:1-2 *Since you have been raised to new life with Christ, set your sights on the realities of heaven, where Christ sits in the place of honor at God's right hand. Think about the things of heaven, not the things of earth.*

Let's look at a few examples of how Holy Spirit engages us in Kingdom living.

1. **Conviction of sin:** The Holy Spirit convinces us of sin. He helps us to recognize when we have done something wrong against God and leads us to repentance. This conviction can come through our

conscience, through the teaching of scripture, or through the counsel of other believers.

2. **Guidance:** The Holy Spirit guides us in our daily lives. He helps us make decisions that are in line with the will of God. This guidance can come through a sense of inner peace or clarity, through the advice of wise mentors, or through signs and circumstances that seem to point us in a certain direction.

3. **Empowerment:** The Holy Spirit empowers us to live a life that is pleasing to God. He gives us the strength and wisdom to overcome challenges and fulfill our purpose. This empowerment can come through spiritual gifts such as prophecy, healing, and discernment, or through the fruit of the Spirit, which includes qualities like love, joy, peace, patience, kindness, goodness, faithfulness, gentleness, and self-control (Galatians 5:22-23).

4. **Unity:** The Holy Spirit unites believers together in the Body of Christ. He creates a community of faith that reflects the Kingdom of God. This unity can be seen in the way that Christians from diverse backgrounds and cultures come together to worship, serve, and support one another, despite their differences. If there is disunity and division happening around you, know that the

enemy has assigned his demons to divide and conquer. Repent from agreeing with him and turn back to the unity of the faith.

5. **Transformation:** Holy Spirit transforms us from the inside out. He helps us to become more like Jesus in our thoughts, attitudes, and actions. This transformation comes through the renewing of our minds, breaking sinful patterns, and the cultivation of virtues like humility and compassion.

PRAY WITH ME: *Father, Your Word commands us to pray without ceasing. That must mean that You empower us with the ability to be aware of your presence consciously throughout our day. What is impossible for us is possible for You.*

DECREE AND DECLARE: *God will keep us in perfect peace as we keep our minds focused on Him.*

Prophecies along the way

Back in church and back in therapy with a wonderfully gifted Christian counselor, I heard God speaking. He wooed and corrected me. My counselor prophesied that I would minister healing to women. When she said it, I remember feeling the rightness of what she was speaking. I knew it would take place and began looking for opportunities to minister and serve women that God placed in my path. My journey soon brought me to many situations where I could be of service. I led Bible studies and orchestrated women's retreats for years.

When I returned to the church, I found myself in a prayer meeting one evening. I decided to share how boring I thought prayer meetings were. I confessed that my mind tended to wander. I really believed that I was the only person who ever struggled with a wandering mind while praying! My pastor's wife boldly prayed and prophesied that I would not only overcome my reticence to pray, but would become a fierce prayer warrior for the Kingdom of God. When I heard her, I laughed. This was not something that resonated with me, but I was determined to not put God in a box. I would say "Yes" to Him when the time came. Years of training followed where I became entrenched in spiritual warfare, declaring and decreeing truth while rebuking and casting down any demonic activity around me or those for whom I was interceding. Today I lead a prayer ministry in my local church. Who would have believed it? Not me; not then.

Chapter Four:
Surrender is key

In the story of my rescue, I touched on how it is very possible to receive Christ as your Savior but not allow Him to be Lord of your life. I lived like that for way too long. I made a mess of my life all the while I was professing to be a Christian. I was in control and making all the decisions. In recovery programs they have a saying: I came to the end of myself. To actually experience the abundant life that God prepared for us, we must come to the end of ourselves.

Matthew 16:24-26 *Then Jesus said to His disciples, Whoever wants to be my disciple must deny themselves and take up their cross and follow me. For whoever wants to save their life will lose it, but whoever loses their life for Me will find it. What good will it be for someone to gain the whole world, yet forfeit their soul? Or what can anyone give in exchange for their soul?*

Surrender brings us to freedom. Seems like a strange thing to say but it is true. When we surrender our will to God's will, we are set free. We are free from expectations we or others try to place on us.

The abundant life starts with surrender. I had to come to the place where I just threw up my hands and gave up running the show. That is when Jesus started putting things back in order. He placed me in a safe place. He blessed my finances and my relationships. My children grew in an environment that worshipped and honored God first. By clearing away the distractions that clogged up my life and mind, God made it possible for me to hear His voice more clearly. We cannot fulfill our destiny if we are walking through life unaware of what is happening all around us spiritually. When we are blind to the unseen realm, we tend to trip over and bump into things, metaphorically speaking. To reach our destination, we have to know where we are going and how we plan to get there.

> Mark 4:11 *To you it has been given to know the mystery of the Kingdom of God.*

If we try to move forward with just our own intellect and reasoning capabilities, we will be moving with only half the information we need to succeed. Our God-given destinies produce eternal fruit. If you thought your destiny was to grow up, pick a career, get married, have children, et cetera, you are missing the mark.

> Ephesians 2:10, *For we are God's handiwork, created in Christ Jesus to do good works, which God prepared in advance for us to do.*

We are Christ's ambassadors, and we have a heavenly purpose for existing here on earth. Listening with our "spiritual ears" is vital to knowing who we really are and what we were put here to do.

Earlier I stated that because we are spiritual beings we will exist forever. Because we now know Jesus, we will be with Him for eternity, but our eternal life does not start when we die. We are in the middle of our eternity right now.

> John 10:10b *I have come that they may have life, and that they may have it more abundantly.*

Let me give you an example of what a day of abundant life might look like. My friend, Jane, wakes up, opens her eyes and smiles. She prays before she rises from her bed. "Good morning, Lord. Thank you for waking me up to a new day." She purposefully does not pick up her cell phone but prepares a cup of coffee and goes to her quiet place to spend the first few minutes of her day with God. She always has her Bible, a journal and her devotionals ready, but this is not a time for habitual reading or journaling. She sits and inquires of the Lord what He would have her do that day. Her thoughts are filled with His answer. Today there will be worship music playing and a few scriptures read. The journal is opened, and she pours out her heart to Jesus. It is not a one-way conversation though. He answers and she writes down what He says. He sometimes gives her direction for how to handle a certain situation. At other times He comforts her and reaffirms His love and care for her. She calls this giving God the "first fruits" of her day.

When this time is finished, Jane (and God because He never leaves her) start the work of the day. Her family and her work need her attention, but God reminds her to also see to her health by making good choices for herself. There are moments of frustration and challenge, but even when she makes the wrong choices, she knows she can focus her gaze again on her Savior, dust herself off, and move on. There is peace here.

Jane knows she is a warrior for God's Kingdom. There are meetings to attend and people to connect with. Community energizes her and helps her move forward in her destiny. There are no perfect days. Some days are harder than others. There is heartbreak and loss within the abundant life. The definition of abundant is: "existing or available in large quantities; plentiful." An abundant life promises a full life. It does not promise a life devoid of pain. An abundant life is a life full - full of both joy and sorrow. The abundant life Jesus promises is also full of His presence along the way. We are not doing this alone. He guides, leads, protects, and empowers.

PRAY WITH ME: *Father, we surrender our own understanding and choose to trust You. Let us choose to believe and embrace Your Word more than what we think or see.*

DECREE AND DECLARE: *The Sovereign Lord will never leave us. He walks with us continually on our kingdom journey.*

Big Sur Days

After learning to differentiate the Holy Spirit's voice from my thoughts or thoughts planted by the enemy, I began to yearn for some time alone with Him. He had freed me from the abusive marriage, and I was hungry to know Him better. I landed a very good job with supervisors that actually allowed mental health days off. Big Sur, California, was only 45 minutes from where I lived. If you've never been there, let me just tell you: the air smells different there – fresher. When you drive through the Eucalyptus trees, just roll your window down and smell. It's amazing – all of it: the trees, the river, the mountains – truly God's country. This is where I would go to be alone with God. I took my Bible and a journal with me, and He met me there every time.

Healing happened. Spiritual growth happened. The closer I got to God, the more I became the person He created me to be.

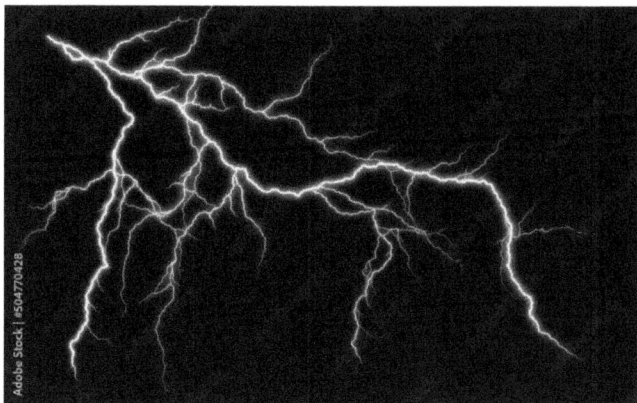

Chapter Five:
The devil is a liar

I know what you may be thinking because I know that the enemy plants thoughts in our minds just like the Holy Spirit does. There are three sources of thought: our spirits, the Holy Spirit, and the demonic. When we receive communication from God in our minds, a demon is right there to discount what the Lord is telling us. I am aware that as you read about the duality of our existence as born-again believers, you may be experiencing thoughts of doubt and resistance to the truth.

Example: The Holy Spirit plants a thought that says, "You are a child of the Most High God and you have a divine destiny." Immediately a thought crosses your mind,

"Who do you think you are? You need to repent from being filled with pride."

This is why it is vital that we study and know the Bible as in 2 Corinthians 10:5.

> 2 Corinthians 10:5 *We demolish arguments and every pretension that sets itself up against the knowledge of God, and we take captive EVERY THOUGHT to make it obedient to Christ.*

Which thought above is rooted in the Word of God? John addresses this.

> 1 John 3:1 *See what great love the Father has lavished on us, that we should be called children of God and that is what we are*!

So, it is clear that the first thought that proclaimed that you are a child of the Most High God is the truth and should be embraced as the truth.

Do not allow the devil to steal your inheritance. He would kill you if he could, but God will not allow him to do so.

PRAY WITH ME: *Father we are so grateful for Your Word. You have not left us without clear direction. Keep us grounded in Your Truth and protect us from the evil one. We pray that we would be full of godly wisdom in the mighty name of Jesus.*

DECREE AND DECLARE: *We serve only Jesus for He is the only truth and the only way.*

Who needs a knight in shining armor?

A couple years after God rescued me, I was on a roll. It was like trying to take a drink from a fire hose. God was speaking and I was trying to drink it all in. I was in church whenever the doors were unlocked. I was speaking at women's groups and facilitating small groups in my home. At one point I decided to facilitate a divorce recovery workshop. I knew how God had rescued me, but I also know how wounded I was. Divorce is like the death of someone who hurt you very badly only they are still alive and capable of causing more harm. On one of my Big Sur days, I remember writing in my journal. *Divorce is like amputation of a diseased arm. You know the arm must be amputated to save your life, but you still miss having your arm.*

We not only studied the Word together, but we went out on outings as a group. One gentleman in our group named John, became a friend. He would buy pizza for the boys and I after Bible study and chat. I was very leery of getting entangled in any romantic relationships. After all, God had rescued me from one bad choice. What made me think I was any wiser in picking a partner now? As my affection for John grew, I started to fervently pray that God would not allow me to be distracted. I was the closest I had ever been to Jesus and the last thing I needed was to be lured away by some man.

During one particular tearful time in prayer, I heard my heavenly Father say, *I am perfectly capable of keeping my place in your life. Trust me to hold onto you.*

I may not have needed a knight in shining armor, but God gave me one anyway. When he asked me to marry him, I said yes. John is anointed to lead our family. He has brought stability and adventure to my life and is my number one cheerleader as I pursue my destiny.

Chapter Six:
The process of maturing

The process by which we grow and mature spiritually is called sanctification. When I became a Christian, I was mentored by more than one person at church who encouraged me to make church a priority and to begin to read and study the Bible. I was also instructed to spend time in prayer – just talking with God and listening for His response. By doing these things I grew to know God better and became able to distinguish His voice in my mind from my own thoughts or thoughts planted by demons.

Father God also uses circumstances in our lives to cause spiritual growth. When we are struggling through a particularly rough season, it is wise to turn our attention to God and His Word. He not only has the answer to every problem, He IS the answer to every problem.

Trees grow strong in strong winds. The wind causes trees to deepen their roots farther into the earth to keep them from being knocked over. During times of great difficulty, we must dig down deep and keep our eyes on Jesus, the author and finisher of our faith. He reveals more of Himself during these seasons. I have heard many believers say that they are grateful for the hard times because it drew them closer to God. Intimacy with the Father is worth our temporary pain.

Toddlers learning to walk fall a lot. They cry for a moment and try again. Spiritually, we are toddlers before we are mature believers. It's okay to get it wrong as we learn to hear and obey God. It is better to be obedient than to do or say nothing and miss the opportunity to partner with God.

PRAY WITH ME: *Father, You are the best parent we could ever hope for. You train us up to be mighty warriors for Your kingdom. Cause us to become the men and women You have created us to be and to fulfill our God-given destinies.*

DECREE AND DECLARE: *His grace is sufficient for us. With God the impossible becomes possible.*

The Big Move

Direction and instruction from the Holy Spirit should encompass our days. As our season of living in California came to a close, circumstances converged to make His will quite plain.

1. We no longer had a church home or a place to serve in ministry.

2. We had dear friends moving from California to Texas so now would be a good time to make the move.

3. John's business could be managed remotely so our income seemed solid regardless of where we lived.

I began to seek God's direction in His Word. I asked for clarity and peace as we wrestled with whether to go or stay. As I read, He consistently spoke words of direction and encouragement as we embarked on this next great adventure. Confirmation after confirmation strengthened our faith and got us through all the road blocks the enemy tried to erect.

In August of 2001 we moved from our home in California to Texas. As you know, on September 11, 2001, the United States was attacked and the whole world changed for us. My husband's company could no longer be managed remotely and we found ourselves without a stable income. If it were not for the many words and promises we had received from God, it would have been very easy to believe we had made a huge mistake. We decided to trust God and stand firm where He had placed us. It soon became very clear that we were exactly where God wanted us for that next season.

Chapter Seven:
Lone wolves need a pack

> Ecclesiastes 4:12 *Though one may be overpowered, two can defend themselves. A cord of three strands is not quickly broken.*

Earlier I spoke about being able to hear the Holy Spirit through mentors and trusted counselors. Sometimes we need to hear it from someone else before we can internalize wisdom. It is dangerous for a Christian to separate themselves from the church. I realize the church is an imperfect institution but that's due in part to us being in it. All our flaws cause our churches to be flawed, but we still need to be a part of it.

> Proverbs 15:22 *Plans fail for lack of counsel, but with many advisors they succeed.*

We need each other. There have been times, too numerous to count, where others have pulled me out of the fire, figuratively speaking. Pray that God keeps your heart softened and that you will always have a teachable spirit.

God created humans because he desired fellowship. We have been created in His image, the Bible says, so we desire community just like He does. When we walk off on our own, it is easy to get lost. When we dismiss the body as being unimportant, we can wander spiritually and miss out on the best God has for us.

> Hebrews 10:24-25 *And let us consider one another in order to stir up love and good works, not forsaking the assembling of ourselves together, as is the manner of some, but exhorting one another, and so much the more as you see the Day approaching.*

Our brothers and sisters in Christ bring us words of encouragement and words of warning. What we bring to the table is equally important. I am being narrow minded and probably self-absorbed when all I can see is how irritating the church can be to ME. If I walk away from the body, I not only lose the wisdom they bring to me, but I am cheating them out of the giftings in my life that can make a difference in theirs.

PRAY WITH ME: *Father, Your Word says that You place the lonely into families. You have created us for community and we are grateful for Your great wisdom in this regard. Protect us from the plans of the enemy to separate us from the church. Keep us linked tightly to one another.*

DECREE AND DECLARE: *We are one body and we will not be separated by strife or division. God's love will knit us together and no plan of the enemy will divide us.*

An Open Door

Just in the past five years I have been given an open door to minister in prayer and intercession like never before. In our church I have leadership that has received my giftings with joy and faith. Our weekly intercession meetings are a place where God rolls back the veil and we see visions and receive instruction.

For example, one night while praying I saw one of our pastors walking around with a target on his back and shared this with the group. The next day he was betrayed by a business partner, and it was clear the enemy was trying to attack his livelihood and distract him from the work of the ministry. Because he was warned, he was not destroyed as the enemy intended.

Another time while in a prayer meeting, we were beseeching God to send warring angels to push back the enemy. Then I saw an angelic army standing shoulder to shoulder in a large auditorium – like a staging area. Suddenly, the doors at one end of the auditorium swung wide open and the army advanced out into the battle. I knew they were there to win it. I saw the immediate answer to our prayers. The Lord showed me what happens in the heavenlies when we pray according to His will.

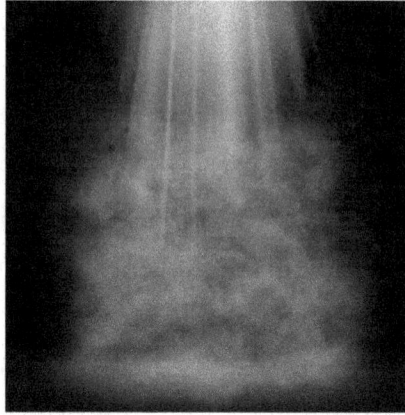

Chapter Eight:
Invisible vs. Visible

We have discussed how we are actually spiritual beings temporarily living in a physical world. If we continue to walk around unaware of the spiritual realm, we miss how much our everyday existence is influenced by the unseen.

> 2 Corinthians 12:2-4 *I know a man that fourteen years ago was caught up to the third heaven. Whether it was in the body or out of the body, I do not know – God knows. And I know that this man was caught up to paradise and heard inexpressible things, things that no one is permitted to tell.*

When we hear God's voice, have prophetic dreams, or see visions that we know are from the Holy Spirit, we are straddling between two worlds. This, as a believer, is our reality.

There is a duality to our lives. We have the capability of washing the dishes and receiving revelation from God simultaneously.

We are living in exciting times. The church is awakening and the people of God are taking their positions. We are watchmen on the wall and warriors on the battlefield. It looks bleak out there, but the enemy will be defeated, and we will be celebrating with Jesus at His victory. We have the capability to be a part of this amazing time in the history of mankind or we can be oblivious to what is going on around us. God always leaves the choice with us.

So, let's Practice! Practice! Practice! Be aware of what God wants to say to us or what He wants to show us. If we are quickly obedient when He asks us to do something or talk to someone, it becomes easier to hear Him the next time. The same is true if we ignore Him. Our ears become dull and we can miss Him altogether.

> 2 Corinthians 5:7 *For we live by faith, not by sight.*

This is not something that just happens immediately after becoming a Christian. In each circumstance we face in life, we have a choice: am I going to choose to believe what God says about me and this situation or am I going to react to what I see with my eyes? I pray we all choose to continue to listen to God. The abundant life is one where we interact both with God and man in peace and harmony. Hopefully, I was able to give you a roadmap on how to get there.

PRAY WITH ME: *Father, You are the author and finisher of our journey. We thank You for allowing us to walk this road with You. You never leave us stranded and we are grateful. This journey You have us on is filled with exciting and wonderful sights and experiences and we wouldn't want to try do travel without You.*

DECLARE AND DECREE: *God goes ahead of us and makes our way straight.*

References

1. Dwight L Moody, "They Said So", 2023
2. Dutch Sheets "Give Him 15", 2023

3. Dutch Sheets and Chuck Pierce "Releasing the Prophetic Destiny of a Nation", 2005

4. Brother Lawrence "The Practice of the Presence of God", 1982

Acknowledgements

First and foremost, I owe everything to my Lord and Savior, **Jesus Christ**. This existence that I experience every day is all due to His love for me and the power of His grace.

My husband, **John Gillaspy**, has been my knight in shining armor and my greatest cheerleader in all the endeavors God puts before me.

My editor, **Jackye Campion**, took these pages and made it a book. Thank you, Jackye, for taking these words of mine and turning them into English. □

Thank you to **DJ Farley** for her inspired cover art. When I have no vision, she is my eyes.

About The Author

Tess Gillaspy lives in Texas with her family and two little dogs. She enjoys living from one air-conditioned living space to another. An active part of her local church, Tess facilitates a weekly intercessory prayer meeting with her husband, John. She trains and oversees teams that pray for those who have been broken by the evil in this world. Her message has been one loud call to freedom in Christ. Tess is passionate about seeing people grow closer to God and become disentangled from habits and behaviors that keep them from being who God created them to be.

If you wish to contact Tess, you may email her at:

TessakaMrsG2@gmail.com

www.ingramcontent.com/pod-product-compliance
Lightning Source LLC
Chambersburg PA
CBHW060431050426
42449CB00009B/2233